Call The Midwife!

Your Backstage Pass to the Era and Making of the PBS TV Series

By Jessica Long

If you like "Call the Midwife", you may enjoy "Downton Abbey" and as a "thank you" for purchasing this book I want to give you a gift. It is 100% absolutely free.

Please go to http://fandomkindlebooks.com/call-the-midwife-bonus/ to claim it.

Disclaimer

All rights reserved. No part of this publication may be reproduced, stored in a retrieval system, or transmitted, in any form or by any means, electronic, mechanical, photocopying, recording or otherwise, without the prior written permission of the author.

Although the author and publisher have made every effort to ensure that the information in this book was correct at press time, the author and publisher do not assume and hereby disclaim any liability to any party for any loss, damage, or disruption caused by errors or omissions, whether such errors or omissions result from negligence, accident, or any other cause.

This book is unofficial and unauthorized. It is not authorized, approved, licensed, or endorsed by Neal Street Productions, the BBC, their writers or producers, or any licensees.

Table of Contents

Introduction 5

Historical Background And Social Context 7
   Historical Background of the East End 7
   Life in the Post-War Poplar Area of the East End 9
   Crime In The East End And The Kray Twins 11
   Workhouses 13
   Disease In The East End 15
   Slums Of The East End 18
   Immigrants In The East End 20
   The Nuns And Midwives Of The East End 21

Background To The Making Of The Drama 23
   Jennifer Worth 23
   Production 24
   Locations 25

Characters and Actors 26
   Sister Julienne – Played by Jenny Agutter 26
      Jenny Agutter 27
   Sister Evangelina – Played by Pam Ferris 28
      Pam Ferris 29
   Sister Bernadette – Played by Laura Main 30
      Laura Main 31
   Sister Monica Joan – Played by Judy Parfitt 32
      Judy Parfitt 33
   Jenny Lee – Played by Jessica Raine 34
      Jessica Raine 35
   Nurse Beatrix 'Trixie' Franklin – Played by Helen George 36
      Helen George 37
   Nurse 'Chummy' Browne – Played by Miranda Hart 38
      Miranda Hart 39
   Nurse Cynthia Miller – Played by Bryony Hannah 40
      Bryony Hannah 41
   Mature Jenny – Narrated by Vanessa Redgrave 42

Conclusion 43

Don't forget to claim your free gift! 45

Introduction

"Call the Midwife" is a BBC (British Broadcasting Corporation) period drama, based on the memoirs of Jennifer Worth. Her trilogy of memoirs, of her life as a midwife and nurse, form the backdrop for the TV show.

Set in the post-war 1950s, it follows newly qualified midwife, Jenny Lee, and the nuns of Nonnatus House.

Nonnatus House is a nursing convent, and part of the Anglican Religious Order, working within the Poplar area of London's East End. Although it administers general medical treatment, the majority of its work is to provide midwifery care, for around 80 to 100 newborns each month.

"Call The Midwife" became an immediate success when it was first aired in the UK in January 2012, and went on to repeat the success stateside when it premiered in the Fall of 2012. It has been taken into the hearts of all who watch it, eager to follow the gritty, post-war stories that both delight and cause heartbreak.

Rivalling the popularity of another period drama, "Downton Abbey", the show has gone from strength to strength, as its fans can't seem to get enough. Currently in its fourth series, it has already been confirmed that a fifth series will follow in 2015.

Join us, as we take a look at its success, the characters and actors, and find out what life was really like in the East End of London in the 1950s. We also go back further to show you the history of the East

End to provide context to East End life as portrayed in "Call The Midwife" and have written this using a rapid-fire organizational concept so that you can quickly get up to speed and glean the information you need as fast as possible.

Spoiler Alert:

Every effort has been made to avoid spoilers for the latest season, Season 3. If you are not current with your viewing of "Call The Midwife", to be sure of not encountering spoilers, I suggest you wait on reading this book until you have reached the end of Season 2.

Historical Background And Social Context

Historical Background of the East End

The East End of London, UK, or simply the "East End" as it is known, is an area of London, east of the medieval walled 'City of London' and North of the River Thames.

The 'East End' is not the same as 'East London', which covers a much wider area.

The River Lea is considered to be the eastern boundary of the East End, although in truth, no real boundaries exist.

Massive expansion in London led to extreme overcrowding, and a concentration of poor people and immigrants in the area, in the centuries prior to the 1950s.

Properties in the East End were typically held on short leases, and so there was little or no development or upkeep in the area.

The building of 'St Katharine Docks', near the Tower of London in 1827, and the central London Railway terminal (1840-1875), exacerbated the problem. Slums were pulled down to make way for the new projects and their displaced residents poured over into the already poor and overcrowded East End.

As a result, the East End became known for its poverty, overcrowding and strong criminal undercurrent.

The term 'East End', used in a derogatory sense, first began in the late 19th century.

Much of the East End, its docks and railways, were destroyed in the Second World War.

The period of the war, known as 'The Blitz', (meaning 'lightning' in German), saw relentless bombing of the East End. Beginning on the 7th September 1940 there were 57 consecutive nights of bombing, causing massive loss of life and damage of homes, workplaces and factories.

After the war, major rebuilding and reconstruction was undertaken. War production quickly changed to making pre-fabricated (prefab) housing for the many thousands of homeless people in the area.

Prefab houses were initially designed to be a temporary solution to the housing problem. However, many were still inhabited years, and sometimes decades, later.

Life in the Post-War Poplar Area of the East End

Although much rebuilding and regeneration was done in the post-war years, it was not enough to deal with the massive housing problem in the East End.

The ruins of bombed houses were still being lived in well into the 1950s. These houses would have walls and roofs missing, and there would be no sanitation, running water, or heating.

Due to new 'regulations' aimed to combat overcrowding, newly built two bedroomed flats could not be let to larger families (of which there were many).

Families too big to be rehoused in properties with these policies had to remain living in squalor. It was not uncommon to see families of 10 or more, living in one or two rooms, with a shared outdoor toilet and a communal tap for water.

Life in the East End was hard and crime was widespread. For those who did manage to find work, wages were low. With no birth control freely available, women tended to have large families, and the mortality rate for both mothers and babies was high.

The gradual arrival of antenatal care in the 1950s put a stop to the needless deaths, through the intervention of hospitals and caesarean sections.

Women would typically enjoy a two week 'lying in' period after giving birth. She would have been

cared for by relatives or neighbors before she resumed 'heavy duties' again.

Sometimes though, older children would be placed in 'foster care' for a week or two, after a new baby arrived. Fathers were not expected to look after children alone, and in the absence of help, other children in the family were sent away.

Crime In The East End And The Kray Twins

The high levels of poverty in the East End have always brought crime with them to the area. One of the most notorious killers in British history, Jack the Ripper, preyed on prostitutes in the area in 1888.

By the 1950s and 1960s, the area was under the criminal control of the Kray twins, Ronnie and Reggie.

They were the head of an organized crime racket that included murder, assaults, arson, armed robberies and an extensive protection racket.

They were born on the 25th October in Hoxton, in the East End.

The boys had a relatively normal childhood, and both took up boxing, a popular hobby for working class boys at that time.

They both proved to be good at boxing, and by the age of 19, they had turned professional.

However, they were already known for their gangs and use of violence to get what they wanted.

In 1952, when enlisting for National Service (mandatory military service), Ronnie punched an army corporal on the chin, severely injuring him. The brothers went on the run, but were later convicted and sentenced to several weeks in prison.

So unruly were they in prison, that the army dishonorably discharged them.

With criminal records and a dishonorable discharge, they were banned from professional boxing, and so their descent into the world of crime began in earnest.

The Krays ruled the East End, and parts of the West End, until the end of the 60s when they were finally caught and convicted. Until then, however, their behavior cast a shadow over life in the East End and caused a notoriety that still exists today.

With their war of intimidation over, many witnesses came forward to testify against them.

They were finally convicted of murder, and sentenced to life imprisonment, with a non-parole term of 30 years. It was the longest sentence ever passed at the Old Bailey in London at that time.

Ronnie remained in Broadmoor Hospital (a high-security psychiatric hospital for the criminally insane), until his death in 1995. Reggie was released on compassionate grounds in 2000, having served more than 30 years. He died 8 weeks later from bowel cancer.

Workhouses

Workhouses originally came into being as early as 1631. They offered a place of accommodation and employment to anyone who couldn't help themselves.

Up until 1834, poor relief was still given to those outside a workhouse, but a new law from this date onwards curbed the opportunity to provide financial help unless the poor entered the workhouse.

It was hoped that with the introduction of this new law, and the influx of free labor that it would provide, workhouses would be able to run at a profit.

However, due the extremely harsh conditions in the workhouses (designed, in part, to discourage people) able-bodied men and women, and therefore those better able to work, tried their best not to enter. The workhouses became a place of last resort, and only the desperate would go there.

By 1929, the general population of the workhouse would be children, elderly, sick, or infirm.

New legislation at this time was brought in to allow local authorities to take over workhouses as municipal hospitals.

Although workhouses were formally abolished in 1930, many workhouses continued to house their population of elderly, young and infirm for years to come while wards for the homeless could be found in most hospitals well into the 1960s.

The workhouse in Poplar was erected in 1735 and stood on the north side of the High Street. In 1757, it relocated to the south side of the street.

Development in the Docks area saw it relocated again, when two new buildings were built in 1815-17.

The workhouse increased in size over the years, and by 1903 it was described as 'a veritable small town'.

In 1913, the workhouse became known as the 'Poplar Institution', and it passed into the hands of the London council in 1930.

The Institution was severely damaged in the Second World War, but its buildings stood on until 1960, when they were finally demolished.

Disease In The East End

With its poverty and slum-like conditions, disease in the East End flourished.

Tuberculosis (or TB) had always been a common problem in the East End, due to the close living conditions and the poor nutrition of its inhabitants, two factors that the disease loves.

A highly infectious disease, TB typically attacks the lungs, although it can affect other parts of the body. Its classic symptoms are; coughing (with blood), night sweats, weight loss and fever.

Being sent away to a sanitarium was the usual treatment for anyone contracting the disease. Recuperation was a long process (often up to a year or more), and the success rate was only about 50%. Some sanitariums were better than others. For instance, those set up for the poor of the community were often no better than a prison, and the survival rate was very low.

The disease was finally brought under control in the 1950s, with a combination of screening, vaccinations and medication.

Rickets was another disease that was prevalent in the East End.

A lack of sunlight and vitamin D, caused by the cramped and slum-like conditions, together with poor nutrition and a lack of calcium in the diet, meant that many, many children suffered with this disease.

Although not fatal, it causes the bones to soften leading to potential fractures or deformities.

Many women who had this disease as a child found that they were now unable to give birth naturally, due to weaknesses in their pelvis. In the days before caesarean sections this meant that many women, and their babies, simply died in childbirth.

Scarlet Fever is an infectious disease that predominately affects children, and was a major problem in the East End.

Scarlet Fever manifests itself in a sore throat, fever and a unique red rash that helped give it its name.

It was brought under control through the use of antibiotics, but before these were introduced, many children died from this disease.

Smog caused a great deal of health problems and was a real problem, not only in London, but also in any built-up town or city.

Before the widespread use of electricity to heat homes, the primary heating source would have been the coal fire.

The smoke from these fires mixed to create a smog so thick that it was often impossible to see more than 10 feet (3 meters) in front of you.

In London, these smogs were known as 'Pea Soupers', and people regularly walked straight into the

River Thames, simply because they couldn't see the water in front of them.

In 1952, a severe spell of cold and windless weather acted with the smoke to cause a smog that descended on London, lasting for five whole days.

Although it caused major disruption at the time, and actually seeped into people's homes, it wasn't considered to be a significant event.

However, later reports showed that 4,000 people had died, and more than 100,000 been taken ill, as a result of the smog and the effects it had on people's respiratory systems.

Research undertaken in more recent years, suggests that the death toll could actually have been closer to 12,000.

It is now known as the worst air pollution event in the UK's history.

As a result, a new 'Clean Air Act' was introduced in 1956. The Act aimed to significantly reduce the pollution, by creating 'smoke control areas' and 'smokeless fuels'.

Slums Of The East End

The slums of London, and the East End in particular, originated in the mid-18th century, when the population of London exploded.

The slum areas of the East End became notorious for their squalor, poverty and crime, and were often referred to as 'The Darkest London'.

During Victorian times, the upper classes would often go on 'slumming' day trips to the East End, where they would marvel at how the lower classes lived, before returning to their own privileged areas of London.

Whitechapel, an area of the East End, just next door to Poplar, was considered the hub of the Victorian East End. It was relatively prosperous at the end of the 17th Century, but by the latter half of the 19th Century, it had become overcrowded and crime-infested.

The East End was, for the most part, ignored and its problems brushed aside by the rest of Victorian London. Most well-heeled Victorians turned a blind eye.

However, by the end of the 19th Century it was a problem that could no longer be ignored, and calls were made for immediate action to be taking in order to improve living conditions.

Slums ceased to be looked upon as a disease and were instead viewed as part of a much bigger social problem.

It took time for this policy to be accepted, but by the 1920s and 30s, slums that were home to around 200,000 people were cleared, and new low cost housing put in their place.

The new housing was built in peripheral areas of London, the idea being to move people out of the East End to relieve the overcrowding.

By the end of the 1930s, the emphasis on new housing had shifted to the building of high-rise blocks of flats instead.

The Second World War put an end to the organized slum clearing. Instead, large areas of the East End were destroyed in the Blitz, something that the planners felt was a blessing.

The truth was a little different though, and it took many post-war years for the area to be cleared of the bombed ruins, and new housing to be put in its place.

Many families lived on in their ruined houses for years after the war, often in a worse condition than they were before the war.

Today, an estimated 10,000 outbuildings are being unlawfully rented out in the East End's 14 square mile (22.5 square km) district alone and overcrowding and poor sanitation are once again proving to be a rising social problem in the area. There are some areas of the East End where the high levels of population have brought the area full circle with its Victorian past of slums.

Immigrants In The East End

The East End has always had a steady stream of immigrants brought to its doors for employment.

Many industries and trades flourished in the area, from as early as Tudor times (15th and 16th centuries).

At first it was just people from more rural areas outside of London who arrived looking for work, but the 17th Century onwards saw many Huguenots (French Protestants) arrive in the East End, and the Spitalfields area in particular.

These were followed by Irish Weavers, Ashkenazi Jews and in the 20th Century, Bangladeshis.

The Nuns And Midwives Of The East End

The National Health Service (NHS) was introduced in 1948 providing the concept of free health care for all, regardless of circumstance or ability to pay, from "cradle to grave".

Before the National Health Service was established, people were, for the most part, expected to pay for their healthcare. The National Insurance Act that had come into effect in 1911, gave basic medical cover to anyone who earned less than £2 per week. However, it wasn't often extended to wives or children, and so the roles of the local community nurses and nuns whose services were free, was invaluable, especially in childbirth.

Typically, only women expecting twins or triplets, or those suffering from complications in pregnancy, would give birth in hospital. Most babies up until 1960s were still birthed in the home.

Although the NHS brought with it free health care, nurses and midwives still played a vital role in the local community. People were initially skeptical of new ideas, and preferred to continue as they had always done.

Poplar and the East End at large was a dangerous place in the 1950s. Crime was prevalent, with the back streets being governed by the notorious 'Kray Twins' (Reggie and Ronnie Kray).

Despite the inherent danger, for the most part, the nurses and nuns were afforded safe passage as they cycled between jobs, often late into the night. Their uniforms gave them protection, as it was widely respected that they were the only help many of the women had when it came to childbirth.

The nuns and nurses tried never to judge and were hugely supportive and broadminded with their patients and their lives. They worked relentlessly, through all weathers, and at all hours, to reach their patients and offer their help.

The order of nuns who worked alongside lay midwives in Poplar back in the Fifties, the Sisters of the Anglican Community of St. John the Divine, are now based in Birmingham, but apparently they never miss a show of "Call The Midwife".

Background To The Making Of The Drama

Jennifer Worth

Jennifer Worth (née Lee) was born on the 25th September 1935 and was a nurse, musician and author.

Her trilogy of books; Call The Midwife, Shadows Of The Workhouse and Farewell To The East End, depict her life as a midwife and nurse in the East End.

Each book has sold over a million copies, making them all best sellers.

Jennifer completed her nursing training in The Royal Berkshire Hospital, Reading, before moving on to London to complete her midwifery training.

Working as a staff nurse at The London Hospital in Whitechapel, she assisted the sisters of St John the Divine, to aid the poor of the community.

Jennifer stayed in nursing for 20 years, finally leaving to pursue her musical aspirations.

In 1974, she was awarded an academic degree with the London College of Music.

She went on to teach piano and singing with the college.

Jennifer passed away in 2011, leaving behind her husband of 48 years and two daughters.

Production

Jennifer's memoirs were sent to film production company, Neal Street Productions, by her agent with a view to having them made into a movie.

The company, owned by celebrated Hollywood director, Sam Mendes, thought it was better suited to an episodic series, rather than a one-off film.

Mendes' business partner, Pippa Harris, loved the books from the outset, but found it difficult to get the series commissioned.

The BBC dragged their heels but in the end, Mendes' stature in the industry counted. All it took was a phone call from him to the BBC and the show went ahead.

They still had to wrangle with the BBC for many months, however, before they got the coveted primetime Sunday evening slot.

The show was an immediate success, pulling in more than 10 million viewers on its first showing in the United Kingdom in January 2012, the highest viewing of a new drama series in over ten years for the BBC.

In the US, the show first aired on PBS in Fall 2012 and records viewership numbers that are 50% higher than average for PBS shows. The third series of "Call The Midwife" aired March 30, 2014.

Locations

Chatham Dockyard in Kent, just south of London, and surrounding locations, are used for much of the filming of the series.

These historical dockyards have been home to the Royal Navy and its fleets since Tudor times, some 400 years or more.

By the reign of Queen Elizabeth I (1558-1603), the Chatham Dockyard had become the main base for the Queen's fleet of ships. It was from here that the Queen's Navy sailed to defeat the Spanish Armada in 1588.

Filming for Nonnatus House, the nursing convent in the series, originally took place at St Joseph's College in Mill Hill, London.

However, by series three the filming had moved to Longcross Studios in Chertsey, Surrey. This was due to the former site of St Joseph's being sold for redevelopment.

Characters and Actors

Sister Julienne – Played by Jenny Agutter

Sister Julienne is the senior nun at Nonnatus House, and the most experienced midwife they have.

Her patience, practicality and deeply held religious beliefs allow her to serve her patients and fellow sisters well.

The other Sisters at Nonnatus House look up to Sister Julienne for her advice and non-judgmental approach. She is often called upon to mediate and maintain the status quo of the largely female environment that they all live and work in.

Sister Julienne's closest relationship is with Sister Bernadette. It is warm and maternal, and Julienne serves as Bernadette's chief mentor and confidante.

Sister Julienne has an almost childlike quality about her. She sees the beauty in everything and nothing is mundane or boring. Although she carries the responsibility of being in charge, she retains a twinkle in her eye and a sense of fun.

Jenny Agutter

Jenny Agutter was born on the 20th December 1952, the daughter of a British Army Officer.

As a child, she lived in both Cyprus and Malaysia (or Malaya as it was known then). On her parents return to the UK, she attended the Elmhurst Ballet School. It was here that she was discovered and given her first acting role, in the film "East of Sudan" in 1964.

She is best known in the UK for her role in the iconic British film "The Railway Children". In the original 1970 version, she plays the role of "Roberta", the eldest daughter. She returned to the film in the 2000 TV version, where she played the role of the mother.

Jenny is also well-known for her role in the 1981 cult classic "American Werewolf in London".

Jenny prepares for her role as Sister Julienne by referring to the notes about her character given to her by the niece of the real Sister Julienne. She says that these notes are 'full and descriptive and give me an image of the person I need to portray'.

Sister Evangelina – Played by Pam Ferris

Sister Evangelina comes from the same background as those she serves in Poplar.

Evangelina grew up in extreme poverty in Reading, a city located south of London. Her upbringing gives Evangelina an insight into the lives of the patients that the nuns and the nurses help. She uses this knowledge to mentor the young midwives and help them feel better equipped to do their job.

She is physically strong and has an enthusiastic sense of humor. Although she gets on easily with everyone she meets, her bluntness sometimes offends others, and lands her in trouble.

She has a delicate relationship with Sister Monica Joan, who comes from an aristocratic background. Their differences of opinion often leaves her at breaking point.

Pam Ferris

Pam Ferris was born in Germany on the 11th May 1948 to Welsh parents. Her father was in the Royal Air Force.

She spent much of her early childhood in Wales, until her family emigrated to New Zealand when she was 13.

Pam has made her career in both TV and on the stage.

From 1991 – 1993, she played the role of 'Ma Larkin' in the British TV classic 'The Darling Buds of May'. The series also starred an unknown (at the time) actress, Catherine Zeta Jones who went on to become an Oscar-winning star, and wife of "Hollywood royalty", Michael Douglas.

Pam has also appeared in film, most notable as "Aunt Marge" in "Harry Potter and the Prisoner of Azkaban".

Not much is known about the life of Sister Evangelina before she became a nun. However, Pam has revealed this about her: 'She's an extraordinarily courageous woman. During the First World War, she was parachuted close to the front line. This was at a time when the survival rate of nurses on the front line, and for anyone parachuting, was 50/50'.

Sister Bernadette – Played by Laura Main

Sister Bernadette is the youngest of the nuns at Nonnatus House.

In her 30s, she is close in age to the other nurses and midwives.

Well educated and a true professional, she teaches the other nurses what she knows, and often offers them advice.

However, she is not completely sure a life in the convent is her true calling, and it becomes apparent that she is lonely.

She turns to Sister Julienne for help after eventually breaking down.

It soon becomes clear that she has fallen in love with Dr. Turner, and after a brief illness with Tuberculosis, she decides to leave the convent, and become a lay nurse and midwife.

She goes on to marry Dr. Turner, and lives with him and her stepson, Timothy.

Laura Main

Born on the 8th March 1981, Laura is a Scottish actress and singer.

She started appearing in musical theatre at the age of 11, and has performed on stage in numerous productions with the Royal Shakespeare Company.

Her big break into TV came with the role of Sister Bernadette.

Sister Monica Joan – Played by Judy Parfitt

Sister Monica Joan was born into a wealthy and prominent family. She was one of the first women to qualify as a midwife, in the latter years of the 19th century.

Becoming a midwife was something of a radical act at the time, and her further decision to become a nun, scandalized her family who never came to terms with her choices.

Her life has been dedicated to providing midwifery services to the poor of the East End.

By the time the 1950s roll around, Sister Monica is in her 90s and retired from nursing. She is still living at Nonnatus house though, and being cared for by her fellow sisters.

Her personality is eccentric and she clashes often with Sister Evangelina. Jenny suspects her eccentricity is more to do with a wilful naughtiness, rather than old age as the other sisters and nurses think.

Sister Monica has a sweet tooth, and will often eat all the cakes at Nonnatus house. The other sisters and nurses take to hiding them from her.

Later in the second series, Sister Monica reunites with her nephew and his family, and it is revealed that her real name is Antonia Cavill.

Judy Parfitt

Born on the 7th November 1935, Judy began her stage career in 1954.

A BAFTA (British Academy of Film and Television Award) nominated actress, she trained at the Royal Academy of Dramatic Art.

She has had a successful career, on stage, TV and in film. She has also appeared on American TV, most notably as the evil stepmother in the series 'The Charmings', and as the mother to Alex Kingston's character in "ER".

Jenny Lee – Played by Jessica Raine

In the show, Jenny starts at Nonnatus House in 1957. Aged just 22, she is totally unprepared for what awaits her.

She has experienced a privileged childhood in the Home Counties (the areas surrounding London), and then went to Paris to train to become a nurse.

Although at first she is shocked at the lives of her patients, she quickly gets used to the poverty, and learns to love both her work and the people who live in the area.

She came to London to escape from her background, as she had fallen in love with a married man named Gerald.

The situation is complicated when Gerald's best friend, Jimmy, arrives and expresses his love for her.

Although she turns him down, they remain friends and Jenny later dates his friend Alex.

Jessica Raine

Born in 1982, the daughter of a farmer, Jessica spent her childhood on a farm in Ross-on-Wye in Herefordshire.

She studied drama at university, but on graduating was turned down at every drama school she applied to.

Jessica then went to Thailand, where she taught English as a second language.

Returning to the UK, she applied to the Royal Academy of Dramatic Art for a second time, and was accepted.

Since graduating in 2008, Jessica appeared on stage, TV and in film before landing the role of Jenny Lee.

Outside "Call The Midwife", Jessica will star in drama "Fortitude," alongside Michael Gambon, Stanley Tucci and Christopher Eccleston in 2014.

Nurse Beatrix 'Trixie' Franklin – Played by Helen George

Nurse Beatrix Franklin, known as Trixie, is already living and working at Nonnatus House when Jenny first arrives.

Glamorous, bubbly and bright, she enjoys jazz, dancing and is a little boy-mad, enjoying setting up her colleagues with dates.

Her easy, no-nonsense approach is a big hit with her patients, and it becomes obvious that work is her first love.

Although Trixie is more outgoing than Jenny, they form a close friendship, sharing the same sense of adventure in their work.

Helen George

Helen graduated from the Royal Academy of Music in London, and went on to study drama at the Birmingham School of Acting.

As a child, she was sporty and had wanted to become a 'long jumper'. However, at the age of 15, after a production of "Les Miserables", she decided that she wanted to pursue a career in musical theatre.

She was a backing singer for Elton John during one his tours, before she landed the role as Trixie.

Nurse 'Chummy' Browne – Played by Miranda Hart

Camilla Chormely-Browne, known as 'Chummy' to her friends, is the daughter of a well-placed family. She has found her way into nursing and midwifery in rather a roundabout way.

Constantly good humored and kind, Chummy is crippled by a lack of self-worth and low self-confidence.

This is due in part to her height and general clumsiness, but also because of her loveless childhood spent in boarding schools.

Chummy is well loved by her friends and colleagues, and by the end of the first season she has dated and married policeman, Peter Noakes.

Season 2 sees Chummy apply for a place as a missionary in Sierra Leone, and her and Peter leave for Africa for 6 months.

When they return, Chummy discovers she is pregnant and despite complications, she gives birth to a baby boy, who they call Fred.

Miranda Hart

Born on the 14th December 1972, Miranda is from an aristocratic family herself, although she doesn't like to admit it.

She can trace her family tree back to the 12th Century and Lullingstone Castle, which is still in the family today.

Her father, David Hart Dyke, was the commanding officer of the HMS Coventry at the time of the Falklands war. The ship was sunk with a loss of 19 lives, and David Hart Dyke was the last person to leave the ship before it went down.

A comedian and actress, Miranda had appeared in various British "sitcoms", before landing the role of Chummy in "Call the Midwife". She is most famous for her own comedy show, "Miranda," in which she plays a similar character to Chummy, a woman who is awkward In matters of life and of the heart, but who is endearing, nonetheless.

Nurse Cynthia Miller – Played by Bryony Hannah

Like Trixie, Cynthia is also a resident at Nonnatus House when Jenny arrives.

Cynthia is caring and intelligent and finds her work rewarding but challenging.

In her early twenties, she quickly forms a firm friendship with Jenny, which goes on to last a lifetime.

Cynthia is the most sensitive of all the midwives, and often gets emotionally involved with her patients, almost always to her own cost.

In season 2, when a baby dies during a childbirth that she is attending, Cynthia blames herself and begins to doubt her own abilities. With the local people pointing the finger at her as well, she suffers a breakdown. Sister Julienne helps her to recover, and an autopsy clears her of any wrong doing when it is discovered that the baby had under-developed lungs.

Bryony Hannah

Bryony was unknown to TV audiences when she won the part of Trixie in 2012.

Prior to that, she won the 2012 Olivier Award for "Best Performance in a Supporting Role" for her part in the London West End stage play, "The Children's Hour". She stole the show even though she was starring alongside Elizabeth Moss ("Mad Men"), Keira Knightley ("Pirates of the Caribbean") and Ellen Burstyn ("Californication").

Bryony trained at the Royal Academy of Dramatic Art in London, is twenty-nine years old, 5'1" tall, and a saxophonist.

Before becoming an actor, Bryony worked in a local pub in her hometown of Portsmouth, and used her wages to fund her trips up to London to appear in fringe theater.

Mature Jenny – Narrated by Vanessa Redgrave

Vanessa narrates the role of the 'mature' Jenny, in the opening and closing of each episode.

Born in 1937, Vanessa is an veteran, and esteemed, actress of both stage and screen.

A member of the 'Redgrave' family of actors, her father Michael, siblings Coran and Lynn, daughters Joely and Natasha Richardson, and niece Jemma are all actors.

Sadly, her father, both siblings and daughter Natasha have all died. Natasha was married to Hollywood actor, Liam Neeson, and died in a skiing accident.

Vanessa has been the recipient of many awards throughout her career. In 2010, she was ranked as the ninth greatest actor of all time, in a poll of industry experts and readers of The Stage (a London weekly entertainment newspaper).

Conclusion

When "Call The Midwife" was first shown on British TV, it had the highest audience of any drama debut in the BBC's history. It went on to become a firm favorite in the States when it premiered there too.

So, why the great success, and just what draws its audience back week after week?

The series shows a side to life that many people didn't realize existed. Most viewers are stunned by the levels of poverty in the East End in the post-war years.

Life was hard and food rationing continued for another 8 to 9 years after the war ended. Work was hard to come by and contraception non-existent at the time so the average size of a family was large.

The series shows a side to life that many people didn't realize existed. Most viewers are stunned by the levels of poverty in the East End in the post-war years.

Women had played a strong role in the war effort, while their husbands had been away fighting. They had become the heads of households, and often the breadwinners. They had taken on roles previously undertaken by men and performed them well. There was a new respect for their skills and abilities.

Even though the men were back from the war, women weren't ready to give up their new found freedom and status. Times were changing, albeit slowly, and the women knew this.

The early Fifties was a time of limbo, if you like. The war was over, but the revolution of the Sixties and the freedoms that it brought (especially to women) had not yet arrived.

The backdrop to all of this is the cycle of birth and death. Women needed to be strong to ensure their own survival and that of their families. The backbone that had seen them through the war and the support networks they had developed were essential to that.

The story lines in "Call The Midwife" are gritty and portray a harsh reality of a time bone by, but not so distant that it stops you from thinking and appreciating what you have today.

Through a mixture of suspense, poignancy, pain and joy, the viewer is drawn into a very female world, and has you hanging onto the edge of your seat waiting for the outcome of each storyline.

The series works because it focuses on very real and identifiable characters. It may be of a time past, and the circumstances of birth may be different today, but the fears, worry and joy are much the same for any new mother now as they have always been.

Don't forget to claim your free gift!

If you like "Call the Midwife", you may enjoy "Downton Abbey" and as a "thank you" for purchasing this book I want to give you a gift. It is 100% absolutely free.

Please go to http://fandomkindlebooks.com/call-the-midwife-bonus/ to claim it.

Printed in Great Britain
by Amazon.co.uk, Ltd.,
Marston Gate.